The Quiet Bride

A Guide to Your Dream Wedding without
Being the Center of Attention

Anita Knapp

~for quiet brides everywhere~

Table of Contents

Are You a Quiet Bride?

Before you buy this book, ask yourself:

- ಹಿ Do crowds exhaust you?
- ಹಿ Have you ever been told you're quiet?
- ಹಿ Do you get anxious in crowds, in front of audiences, or in new spaces?
- ಹಿ Do you consider yourself to be a wallflower, an introvert, or a "quiet person"?
- ಹಿ In your group of friends, are you the "good listener"?
- ಹಿ Would you rather curl up with a good book and a cup of tea than go to a party?
- ಹಿ Does the thought of getting married make you anxious?

If you answered "yes" to any of these questions, then this book is for you!

Introduction

Hello beautiful bride-to-be! First of all, congratulations! Secondly, I want to thank you for picking up this book. Knowing you need it is actually the first step in the right direction towards the wedding of YOUR dreams, on YOUR terms. As an introvert, I finally found bravery in anonymity and decided to write this book using a pen name (sorry, Anita Knapp is not my real name), so I can share what I learned while going through the process to get the wedding my husband and I wanted.

This is important: YOU MATTER. YOUR OPINIONS MATTER. In fact, YOUR DESIRES are the BOTTOM LINE. Please let that sink in. This is your wedding, your day, and your dream. I have an important message for dear relatives in the next section who might feel otherwise, so please share it with them.

Now, about this book. *The Quiet Bride* is designed with you in mind! Not all introverts are the same, and not everyone reading this book is necessarily a "classic introvert". There are many reasons why a bride might not what to follow wedding traditions and this book is meant to offer alternatives and help inspire confidence. You can use as much or as little as you need. For example, if the entire idea of a traditional wedding has you in a panic, you should read all of it. Or, if you have no idea what to do about your fear of dancing in public, skip ahead to Chapter Three: Receptions for help with that.

As the author, I have two central goals with this book:

1. Provide you, the bride, with classy, tactful alternatives to many wedding traditions, as well as subtle things you can do to help yourself get through your wedding

2. Give you the confidence and assurance you may need to follow through with your wishes

When I first got engaged, I went to the library and checked out every single book on wedding planning they had, even the ones from the 80's! I read them *all*. Then, I ordered more. Crowds exhaust me. Audiences send me into a panic. Loud music gives me a headache. You see, after I read all those wedding planning books, I had this idea of what I *had to* do for my wedding, and it made me miserable! I shut down—I didn't want to plan anymore, I just wanted to elope (which we almost did).

Then, I scoured the Internet for tips for people like me. And that's what I got—tons of blogs and websites with a few tips each, no book or single resource. Many of the tips involved things *I* had to do personally in order to survive my own wedding, a "grin and bear it" approach that suggested the uncomfortable aspects of a wedding are entirely unavoidable.

Thankfully, I had the time and willpower to read all that advice, but you might not. That's why I wrote this book. I'm taking what I learned, plus a lot of extra research, and compiling it into one, focused book that is easy for you to go through page by page, or as you need. Additionally, many of the things I include are not things you have to do in order to "get through" your day. Your wedding day shouldn't feel like a marathon or presentation, it should be the best, most care-free day of your life.

In this day and age of bigger and louder weddings, you may feel pressured to conform. This pressure can come from within, or it can come from your friends and family. They might not even realize they're doing it! I'm here to tell you that you *can* be a quiet bride and you *can* have a quiet wedding, if you wish. If bigger and louder is what you want, there are tips in this book to offer that experience to your guests while maintaining your sanity.

Some of the advice in this book may come across as mean or selfish. However, after decades (if not centuries) of mild mannered women putting up with uncomfortable ceremonies and celebrations because that's the "norm", I think it's high time for a revolution! A *quiet* revolution.

Though I do my best to consider your guests' feelings and tastes, my primary concern is *you*, the bride. I may sound pushy at times, but that's because I feel it's necessary. I wish someone had taken me by the bootstraps and said in a firm, reasonable tone, "No, you don't need to do this and you don't need to do that, you need to be yourself!"

"Quiet people have the loudest minds."
–Stephen Hawking

Just because you're quiet doesn't mean you don't have opinions. I reiterate this a few times throughout the book, because it's important. Your friends and family may be used to interpreting your silence as acceptance or apathy, but try not to let them do that when it comes to your wedding.

I'm so happy for you! I wish you the best for your wedding and your future together with the person of your dreams. I hope this book can help you get there with ease, happiness, and fun.

Much Love,

Anita

A Note to Loved Ones

Dear mothers, grandmothers, future mother-in-laws, future grandmother-in-laws, sisters, future sister-in laws, best friends, long-lost friends, relatives, and any other person (guy or gal) involved in the bridal party and/or wedding planning,

If you are reading this, it's because a bride you know feels like you need to. This is a gentle reminder to shift your focus back to the bride. Her wishes may not align with your dreams or plans, and that's just fine. It's her day. She has her own dreams, and it's your job to listen to and support her dreams. You may feel you know what's best, especially if you've been down the aisle before, but it's not about what's "best". Please let that sink in.

I'm going to assume you love the bride, so please listen to her. If you know her well then you might already be aware that she sometimes keeps her opinions to herself, because that's the most comfortable. So be patient! Be encouraging, but not demanding. Take time to listen, actually listen. The bride may be a really good listener because she's spent a lifetime avoiding the spotlight, encouraging others to talk so she won't have to.

She may be the woman you turn to when you need to vent.

While wedding planning can be a delight, it's also a huge stress, especially for the bride. Please take a moment, and you might need to do this once a week, to shed your personal desires for the wedding. It's the bride's wedding, and the reason she picked this book up is to help her get through it happy and stress-free (or as low-stress as possible!), so that she can look back on her day with feelings of joy rather than regret.

Love,

Anita

The Quiet Bride

Chapter One:
It's All in the Details

Use subtle cues to help your guests take a hint.
From color psychology to strategic placement, here
are some things you can control to help manage
your crowd. This chapter is for brides who want to
reign in a large group of loved ones…without ever
having to say a thing!

Timing

This is the biggest hint you can offer to your
guests, as well as the most obvious. You've
probably heard that avoiding Saturday weddings
will save you money, but it will also save you noise
and drama. Thursday, Friday, and Saturday nights
are usually reserved for partying. Saturday
weddings, especially with evening receptions, are
almost expected to be loud parties with
enthusiastic DJ's and open bars. So, if you must

marry on a Saturday, opt for a late morning or early afternoon.

A ceremony at 10:00 A.M. followed by brunch is totally an option, as is a 1:00 P.M. ceremony followed by a dessert bar. Sunday weddings are gaining popularity, as are weddings on other days of the week. In addition to smaller crowds, you will likely save money. Yes, planning a non-Saturday wedding is seen as a little snub-ish, but if you need permission, here it is: go right ahead!

Avoid holidays. Independence Day, Christmas, New Years, and others are associated with parties, so steer clear of dates that are already on the calendar.

Language

Behold! The power of words. Is there really much of a difference between "party" and "celebration" or "gathering" and "get-together"? Yes! Choose your words wisely to get the message to your guests, indirectly.

Utilize a thesaurus to find milder versions of the words you want to use. Say them aloud and write down what kind of imagery those words create. Try them out on your fiancé, family, and friends.

Typography

Even subtleties like the fonts you use can offer hints on the kind of gathering you're having. I would suggest working with a skilled graphic designer on your announcements, invitations, and programs, but here are some tips you can follow if you're doing things yourself:

- ❧ Stick with classic, easy to read serif fonts and script. This book uses Book Antiqua, which would be a safe option.
- ❧ Use fonts that are spaced closer together to hint at intimacy
- ❧ Keep it uniform: use no more than two fonts, otherwise it's too busy

Colors

Color Psychology is your friend! If you have your heart set on some colors already, take a look at what kinds of feelings those colors can evoke. Of course, there are dozens of shades in between which may change the effect. You may also need to consider the season when picking your colors, since an "off-season" color could stick out and null its calming benefit.

Warm colors tend to inspire energy, while cool colors encourage tranquility. There are exceptions, of course, and finding a combination that you and your fiancé agree on may be stressful, but a good combination truly will make all the difference on your wedding day.

Red: the color of passion and aggression. There aren't many shades of red that would inspire quieter reactions from guests.

Pink: pale pinks are associated with youth, sweetness, and femininity, and traditionally signify sincerity. Hot pink is loud and energetic. Stick with the paler shades, like powder pink.

Coral: this pinky-orange shade is making a comeback, and evokes friendly, care-free feelings.

Orange: today, orange is seen as spirited and inviting. To get that feeling, but relaxed, try peach.

Yellow: yellow is a very energizing color that signifies happiness. Pair a lighter shade of yellow with a neutral to tone it down.

Green: this largely neutral color has a negative connotation with envy, but it also positively signifies nature, life, and steadfastness. From mint to olive, there are many shades that will help keep your guests calm. Avoid lime.

Turquoise: a bright combination of green and blue, turquoise is both quirky and friendly. Pair with a neutral to rein in this color's energy.

Blue: the calmest color of them all, in the right shades. Blue represents tranquility and commands respect, and traditionally symbolizes masculinity. Stick to less saturated shades to attain blue's calming effect, though pair it with a neutral or warmer hue to avoid a potentially depressing combination.

Navy: the darkest blue possible, navy is a classic choice that symbolizes sophistication. Avoid pairing with white or ivory to lessen sharp contrasts.

Purple: a combination of red's passion and blue's serenity, purple is a traditionally royal color and symbolizes richness. Lighter shades are romantic and light-hearted, while darker shades are majestic.

Gold: there is nothing subtle about gold! It literally signifies wealth and prosperity. If you want gold, tone it down with a matte version.

Silver: gold's understated sister is milder and more sophisticated. Use silver if you want some subtle sparkle and shine.

Black: the most formal color, black is sophisticated and powerful. It contrasts sharply with any other choice, which can be stimulating and intimidating.

Gray: neutral and muted, gray can either present as cold or calming, depending on what it's paired with. An excellent option for quiet brides if used carefully.

Brown: the color of earth and chocolate. Brown represents loyalty and comfort. This rich neutral color is a good choice for autumn weddings.

Beige: this color has been in and out of popularity and represents warm neutrality.

Ivory: a warmer, elegant version of white, ivory is one of the best choices for quiet brides. It evokes white's purity, but softened, which will leave your guests feeling calm and hopeful.

White: bright white is pure and signifies cleanliness, but it can also appear sterile. By itself white is not stimulating, but if it's contrasted with darker colors, it could be. If possible, use ivory instead.

Winning combinations that are both calming and aesthetically pleasing: mint and coral, powder blue and silver, lavender and ivory, and gray and deep bronze.

Final Notes on Color: avoid sharply contrasting combinations, which are visually stimulating. Navy and white wouldn't work too well together, but steel blue and ivory would.

Flowers

The language of flowers has a long history. Skilled florists are fluent in the different meanings of all the blooms, so make sure to discuss that during your consultation. More importantly, be sure she understands your wedding desires. You don't need to sacrifice beauty in order to achieve a look that encourages your guests to remain calm. Use words like elegant, simple, uniform, and contained to give her an idea of the kinds of arrangements you want.

Blooms to consider include: calla lilies, roses and spray roses, ranunculus, tulips, waxflowers, freesia, lily-of-the-valley, and anemones. You may want to avoid orchids, Gerbera daisies, daffodils, other lilies, and sunflowers, since they tend to be larger and/or more visually interesting.

Patterns and predictability are calming, so avoid putting a unique arrangement on every table or giving each bridesmaid a unique bouquet. Again, this doesn't have to translate as boring! Just avoid wild, artistic arrangements with large, attention-grabbing blooms.

Use the color list to pick out colors that align with your personality and needs. Although flowers can come in more colors now than they could a generation ago, there are still some limits, so it's best to be a little flexible.

Consider using calming herbs, such as lavender, rosemary, and chamomile, in your arrangements to promote a calm atmosphere. Tip: adding peppermint to your own bouquet can help keep you focused and reduce stress, though it is a bit more stimulating so you may want to keep it away from your guests.

Décor

I've been to many weddings where photos of the couple, together and separate, decorate every surface imaginable, or they play on a looped slideshow for hours. I knew right away that would make me uncomfortable, so we didn't do it. Even though your wedding is the pinnacle point of you and your fiancé's relationship, there are other ways to celebrate it without plastering your faces everywhere.

Ask yourselves these questions:

- ℰ What makes you, as a couple, unique?
- ℰ What are your fondest memories?
- ℰ What are your favorite things to do?

- ✤ What have you taught each other?
- ✤ How have you made one another better people?

You can take the focus off of your faces and images and instead direct your guests' attention to meaningful items or representations of your memories. For example, replicate the signage of the place he proposed, or pull inspiration from the place you met each other for the first time.

On the other hand, you don' need to "personalize" your decorations at all! It's perfectly acceptable to stick to the standards (tulle, candles, drapes, balloons, etc. in your wedding colors), or this is another area where creativity can come in handy. As an alternative to the "uniform" look (which is calming on a psychological level), you can distract your guests with inventive and intricate table decorations, so they spend more time staring at them than you!

Music

Music is powerful. It can inspire emotions in ways like nothing else can. If you're aiming to keep your crowd quiet, stick to slow, ambient music such as orchestral ("classical"), acoustic versions of your favorites, or even a live quartet, which has the bonus of providing another distraction for your guests. You can also think outside the box and pull songs from movie scores, videogame scores, or you could even hire a composer to create something new just for your wedding!

If you're hiring a DJ, make sure he knows this is not a typical wedding. You want to keep the crowd mellow. However, mellow doesn't *have* to mean slow, ambient music — you can give folk rock a try to create a more upbeat atmosphere without over-doing it.

Seating

Crowd management psychology tells us to avoid creating spaces where crowds can gather, to create clear pathways for traffic, and give people enough individual space so they stay spread out.

When setting up seating, think "space" and "uniformity". Though it may seem counterproductive to spread people out as far as possible, the closer people are packed together, the more trapped you'll feel. If you're using round tables that can fit six to eight people per table, seat for six. Do both you and your guests a kindness by requesting that your reception set up is accessible — not only will this give you the space you need, but it will make it easier for all your guests to navigate regardless of their abilities.

Round tables are the best option because it's very easy to set them up in a uniform way. Patterns and predictability are calming, so avoid "artistic" set-ups. Opt out of a sweetheart table or a platform, since that will just make you and your new husband stand out. If you feel like you should set you and your bridal party apart a little, use a different color table cloth or a slightly larger version of your centerpieces.

Summary

There are a lot of tricks you can utilize to create the kind of atmosphere you want, and the kind of crowd you want. The first option isn't always the best option, so take your time planning and communicating with those involved in your wedding and reception. Do your research and go in armed with knowledge! Your guests won't even know what hit them.

Chapter Two:
Ceremonies

This chapter covers your options for a wide variety of wedding ceremonies. From courthouse nuptials to Catholic masses, read this chapter for tips on how to tie the knot without battling performance anxiety.

For All Ceremonies

What do you and your fiancé *really* want? Focus on that. If you're worried about "what's expected" of you, *why* are you worried and *why* are you considering others' expectations? This is one of the times I'm going to tell you to listen to your heart, and your fiancé's heart, too. It's a very nice gesture to follow a family tradition or a loved one's wishes, but if it's going to cause you anxiety or regret, it's honestly not worth it. Let me repeat that:

your wishes and feelings are the most important on *your* wedding day.

Unfortunately, unless you choose the courthouse route, you're going to have to endure the spotlight for at least a little while during the actual ceremony. See Chapter Seven: The "Quiet Bride" Look for ideas on how to discourage guests from staring at you, even though you stand out as the bride.

Remember, this day will live the longest in your and your fiancé's memories, so do what is best for you. Trust me when I say that many, many brides wish they'd done what they wanted instead of followed others' wishes. It saddens them that the dominant feeling when they think of their weddings is regret! I can tell you personally that it's a *very* good feeling to look back on my wedding day with feelings of satisfaction and bliss.

Consider the Courthouse

In addition to saving a lot of money, keeping things civil will save you the most stress. There are no guests, no long ceremonies, and no awkward and public declarations of love. And you can do it whenever you want! Skip a ceremony altogether and host a reception to celebrate your new union.

In the United States, laws and requirements usually differ from county to county and state to state, so research carefully if you decide this route. You may need to wait a week or more in between applying and signing, and not every courthouse offers an officiant on site. Check with the county where you want to be married well ahead of time to avoid rushing and making mistakes.

Keep it Short and Sweet

Your best bet is to simply keep the ceremony as short as possible. Smaller wedding parties help with this, and skipping some of the traditional parts. An easy way to shorten the ceremony is for you and your fiancé to go through your officiant's typical ceremony and weed out what isn't meaningful to you as a couple. Don't go through the charades at your own expense if they aren't important to you!

Do you really need three different readings, or will a single poem do? Does lighting a unity candle feel awkward? Skip it! You can write your own (short) vows or pick one of the shorter versions of the traditional vows. Frankly, the less time you have to spend in front of your crowd, the better. Take a critical look at your ceremony plans instead of assuming you "need to" do everything your Cousin Tina or BFF Kayla did. You may raise eyebrows when you tell your officiant, "No thanks," to some things, but be firm: many parts of the ceremony are traditional and are *not required*.

"Intimate" is Always an Option

Another option for any ceremony is to invite fewer people. Maybe you just want immediate family and a few friends at the ceremony. You can always invite more people to the reception. If anyone complains, simply say that space or fire code was an issue.

Yes, some people might be hurt that they weren't invited to the ceremony, but if they can't understand why you would want a more intimate ceremony, then they aren't the kind of person you would want there anyway. Simply accept that you can't please everyone, and move on. Make sure they get their fill of cake at the reception and all will be well!

Front and Center

Does the idea of walking down the aisle terrify you? Don't do it! A new trend is for the bride and groom to each enter from the sides, and walk towards each other. This may not work for every church or venue, but it's an option to consider.

Instead of facing each other once you make your way to the altar, angle yourself toward the officiant. This way you take your eyes away from the crowd and can focus more on the ceremony itself, and the crowd still has a nice view of you.

Religious Considerations

If you practice a certain faith, you're probably very familiar with its traditions by now. However, it can't hurt to do some research and get outside opinions on what's "allowed" and what's frowned upon, since the way your church does things may not be the only way. If you're marrying into a different faith, or combining faiths, you definitely need to do your research! Some religions are very strict in their ceremony requirements; for example, a Catholic ceremony needs to take place in a Catholic church (though permission to marry elsewhere, including outside, is possible).

If the person performing the ceremony is someone you've known your whole life, you may feel very comfortable discussing your plans, which is great! On the other hand, this person may *think* he knows what you want, and may be quite surprised if you voice a different opinion.

Today there is a lot more flexibility in marriage ceremonies, and inter-faith ceremonies are more common than ever. Even if you come from a very strict religious background, likely there is some wiggle room to help make the ceremony the most comfortable for you and your fiancé. Remember, creativity is key and may help you find some solutions to sensitive religious issues.

Non-Denominational

The sky is the limit! This is a great option for doing whatever will make you the most comfortable. Plus, it's a great solution if your and your fiancé's families practice different religions (or no religion at all).

With a non-denominational ceremony, any person who is a registered officiant can perform the marriage. This is a great option for quiet brides who are intimidated by religious leaders, or any person of authority, because a close friend or family member can become an officiant. It's quite easy to become ordained; in fact, a few dollars and a few minutes on the Internet is all it takes!

Summary

There are many ways to tie the knot in this day and age, more than ever before. Even if you think you know what you want, take time to research your options. You may find an idea or two that will make your wedding day even better!

Chapter Three:
Receptions

Time to party…or not! This chapter is all about the wide range of receptions seen today, and which of those is most comfortable for quiet brides. From potlucks to catered seven-course meals, there are plenty of options to fit your and your guests' needs and tastes. If you already know what you want, feel free to skip this chapter.

Reminder on Seating: remember in Chapter One: It's All in the Details, when we discussed strategic seating? Feel free to go back and re-read that section, but the essential rule is to keep seating uniform and to spread everyone out as much as possible. This keeps you out of the spotlight and makes it a bit more difficult for your guests to pack in and create that "trapped" feeling that tends to come with crowds.

There Aren't Any Rules

The first rule is…there really aren't any! This is a great time to be a quiet bride because so many couples are tossing convention to the wind, leaving us with plenty of license to do what's best for our quiet natures. From picnics to formal dinners and everything in between, there are many ways to celebrate your union with your guests.

Food

According to my older relatives (and the experts), wedding receptions didn't used to consist of huge dinners and dances. Light beverages and a few snacks along with a wedding cake used to be the norm! It was only after getting married became an industry that the "bigger is better" mantra came along. Here are several different ideas for food options, listed in order from least to most potential stress.

Light Refreshments: yes, it's still an option! This may not be a popular option, but it's a legitimate one. You can even provide refreshments yourself to save money, or hire a caterer for a more professional feel. Light refreshments typically means a few hot and cold beverages (like tea, coffee, lemonade, punch, and alcohol if you desire), sweet and savory snacks or appetizers, and of course the wedding cake or cupcakes. You may be able to pull this option off at the ceremony site in order to save more time. The great thing about this option is that there usually isn't assigned seating, so guests aren't encouraged to linger.

Dessert Bar: similar to light refreshments, a dessert bar (or a fruit bar, breakfast bar, bacon bar...you get the idea) consists of a limited amount of food and drink and unassigned seating, if any. For this option, include a few different hot and cold drinks, your favorite desserts as a couple, and the wedding cake or cupcakes. Again, you can probably pull this off yourself or you can cater with a local bakery. With the light refreshments and dessert bar options, you have the freedom to move around and get away for a few minutes, when you need to.

Brunch: do you like the idea of a meal, but not a dinner? Brunch is the happy medium! The best part is that you don't necessarily need to do a brunch in the late morning, though that's probably what your guests will expect. Brunch can be dressed up or down depending on your vision—

include mimosas and a juice bar for a more sophisticated feel, or have pancakes with whipped cream and sprinkles to bring out everyone's inner child. Brunch is a fun meal that has an end in sight: you're guests won't stick around to party afterword, but they'll feel like they had a good time.

Pot Luck or Picnic: if you're comfortable with a lot of people in an informal setting, a pot luck or picnic is a safe choice. These options are considered very casual, so if you choose one, be sure to indicate on your invitations that guests should dress appropriately. The great thing about a pot luck or picnic is the flexibility!

Buffet Meal: one of the two common choices for modern receptions is a buffet-style dinner, with one or two lines for guests to walk through. They can either serve themselves or sometimes staff, either with the catering company or the venue, will serve. Buffet dinners are slightly less formal and will probably keep guests focused on the food a little more, since they have to make the effort to get it.

Seated Dinner: this is the most formal option for a modern reception. This is the least ideal situation, since guests are seated and able to concentrate on their surroundings. Guests will expect speeches during this time, but another form of entertainment could work in this situation, such as a quartet or other musical act. If you can afford it, look into other entertainment options to keep your guests focused on something other than you.

Alcohol

Liquid courage, or liquid instigator? Yes, I'm talking about alcohol. I mentioned earlier that many wedding guests expect alcohol to be served at a reception, oftentimes in the "open bar" set up. Does this mean you have to cater to that expectation? Not necessarily. There are several arguments in favor and against serving alcohol at a wedding. Ultimately, do whatever makes you feel the most comfortable.

Since serving alcohol is the norm, here are some good reasons to stay "dry" instead:

ɞ It will be quieter. Nothing increases volume like alcohol!

ᘂ It will be much safer. Guests can't drive home drunk if they're sober.

ᘂ It will probably be less dramatic. Nothing starts fights like drunken insults hurled by relatives and strangers alike.

ᘂ Finally, you'll save a lot of money.

This is a good time for some self-evaluation. Do you usually indulge in alcohol to make social interactions a little easier? You definitely aren't alone! Many people feel like they can't function at a party unless they're imbibing in an adult beverage (or two or three…) Does the thought of getting through your wedding *without* alcohol make your stomach churn with nerves? You may have a deeper issue that *The Quiet Bride* won't be able to solve. If this sounds like you, *please* seek help.

The Grand Entrance

"Introooooducing, Mr. and Mrs. Happy Couple!" shouts the DJ! Or not. This is another thing the guests will likely expect if you're going the "party" route, but you don't need to do it if it makes you uncomfortable. Instead of your bridal party going in couple by couple, enter as a group.

Better yet, don't make a scene at all. Just melt into the reception like you've been there all along. It really depends on the venue and the type of reception you're having. Here's my permission to skip the grand entrance if you want to.

Receiving Line

This is one way to avoid the grand entrance. Traditionally, the receiving line can take place either immediately following the ceremony, or at the beginning of the reception. I recommend doing it at the reception because you will already be overwhelmed at the ceremony, and then you can take an extended break after.

A receiving line is exhausting and would probably be the most difficult part of your wedding day, if you choose to host one. Regardless of the number of guests, the sheer repetitiveness of greeting them will soon wear you out (even though you love them and you're happy they could attend). Actually focusing on each individual person can help you stay grounded and can alleviate the sensation that you're on an assembly line.

Other ideas include ditching the "line" completely in favor of a cocktail hour, or dismissing your guests individually from the ceremony instead. Feel free to get creative if you know you won't be able to handle a receiving line. Or, ditch it completely!

Speeches

I admit it, I've heard some great speeches that brought tears to my eyes, and I've heard others that were painfully awkward. A great speech depends on the speaker, but either way you're going to be the focus of the speech, so there's no way to dodge the spotlight.

A way around this is to forgo the speeches and opt for something creative instead, enlisting the help of your maid of honor and best man to steal the show:

- Have them make a speech together, which will be different enough to shift the focus away from you and make your guests wonder what the speakers are up to.
- Instruct them to launch a lantern (if you're outside) in your honor. All eyes should be on the lantern.
- Let them think outside the box! If they know you well, they will understand your plight and

likely be more than willing to try something different in order to make you more comfortable.

Clink, Clink, Clink, Kiss!

It's probably going to happen, no matter what you do to try and prevent it. If you're fine stopping whatever you're doing (eating, drinking, breathing, or talking) and kissing your new husband, then go ahead and skip this part. But if you want to avoid this tradition, for whatever reason, you can try a few different things to dissuade guests from attacking their wine glasses with forks:

ဢ Signage. Whether you place notices in your program, on the tables, or hang signs from the ceiling, you can try to appeal to your guests' reasonable side. You can go for a serious tone, or try something humorous ("Stop glassware violence!"), but it should stop at least some of your guests.

ဢ Make it a challenge for them. Instead of clinking glasses, make them sing a song, play rock, paper, scissors, or make their glasses resonate (run a wet fingertip around the rim)

ଛ Enlist the help of your bridal party. If some or all of them are willing, once the clinking starts send them out to kiss the clinker…it probably won't happen again.

ଛ Don't give them the satisfaction. Get a large fan or parasol and hide behind it with your husband when you hear clinking. If people boo, have your bridal party glare at them. All in good fun, of course.

ଛ Don't be afraid to get creative! Couples are doing all sorts of quirky and fun things to avoid this tradition.

Cutting the Cake

Whether you're going the traditional route with a silver knife or not, at some point your guests will expect you and your new husband to shove cake in each other's faces. You may be looking forward to this, but if you aren't, just skip it! This is one wedding tradition (signifying the couples promise to provide for one another) that is on its way out. Here are several alternatives to a traditional wedding cake:

ଛ Keep the topper solely as a decoration

- Have a cake table, with a variety of smaller cakes (your favorites, of course!)
- One hot trend is cupcake towers, with either regular or mini cupcakes in a variety of flavors
- Have a dessert bar with several different kinds of desserts (or ice cream, candy, cookies…)
- Start with a huge, plain white cake and allow your guests to decorate it. Similarly, allow them to decorate their cupcakes.

Dance

My husband and I hate dancing, so we didn't host a dance. That's always an option for you! This is a personal observation, but I haven't been to a wedding where the dance floor hasn't felt awkward in some way, or the DJ hasn't felt pushy. That might just happen to be my experience, so I'm willing to give dances the benefit of the doubt. If you want a dance, or feel like it's something you need to include, go ahead! Here are some tips for surviving the traditional dances:

First Dance: you don't have to do it alone. A nice way to follow the tradition but bow out early is to do an Anniversary Dance instead. You and your new husband join all the married couples, and the

DJ eliminates couples (as the newlyweds, you get to leave the dance floor first!) until those married the longest remain. As a bonus, the attention is on them instead. Other ideas for a "first" in lieu of a dance altogether include: drink, game (video or board), jump in a bouncy house, karaoke…you can totally do whatever you want. Seriously.

Father-Daughter, Mother-Son Dances: as with the first dance, you don't have to do a dance at all! Depending on the kind of relationship you have with your dad (or whoever you would do this with), you can do something totally creative, within your comfort zone. Have a heart-to-heart with your dad. Maybe he's been looking forward to this dance since you were born, or maybe he's been dreading it, too.

The Dollar Dance: I do not see how any quiet bride would be comfortable doing the Dollar Dance (where guests pay to dance briefly with you), but if you want to do it or need the cash, do ahead! Otherwise, nix it with my blessing.

Have a Themed Dance

If modern dances aren't your thing, but you still want to dance, take it back a few decades. Select music from a single decade, or pick a theme like swing or early rock n' roll. Your guests will probably love the change, especially if you provide some fun favors for them to fit in. You could also build your theme around a movie or destination...or get creative!

The Garter Toss

I'll be honest—I've never watched this part of the reception go down without cringing. It's awkward at best and vulgar at worst. I don't imagine many quiet brides would be comfortable with this tradition, so feel free to skip it.

However, if you feel like you need to include *something* with your garter, give it to your groom ahead of time. Take a seat and pretend like you're getting ready for it, then have him pat himself on the chest, find the garter in his pocket, and say something like, "Oh, how did that get there?" Not only will you get a few laughs and raised brows, but the attention will be on him, instead.

The Bouquet Toss

This is one tradition that can cause serious injury, from high heels puncturing feet to elbows banging noses. Something else to consider is that not all the single ladies like to be reminded that they're single (or unmarried, depending on your wording), or they don't like feeling pressured to reveal that they are. However, if this is something you want to do, go right ahead! It can be really fun.

On the other hand, here are some alternatives:

- ❧ Give your bouquet to someone special, to honor him or her
- ❧ If you do the Anniversary Dance, you could give your bouquet to the couple who has been married the longest
- ❧ Have an "exploding bouquet": make an identical version of your bouquet, but comprised of several mini bouquets you can either give out individually, or throw in their air for a flower explosion
- ❧ Alternatively, you could completely dismantle your bouquet and give out individual flowers

ဏ Forget flowers altogether and throw lottery tickets, candies, and other fun things so that everyone is a winner!

Note: You may want to alleviate pressure from the garter and bouquet catchers by forgoing that other awkward tradition. Last time I checked, most girls don't really like a strange guy slipping a garter onto their legs. If you still want to honor this tradition, have them take a picture together, or see who can shoot the garter the farthest, or something entirely new!

Photo Booth

This is a great way to give your guests an activity to do that will also result in a memento for them. You can set one up yourself with a backdrop and tripod (with plenty of props, of course!), or you can hire a photo booth package. They are gaining popularity and more than likely you'll have a few options in your area. If you have a theme, make sure to supply props that go with it!

Summary

Receptions, like ceremonies, can take almost any form these days. Whether you're sticking with formal or going casual, there are literally dozens (if not hundreds) of ways to put a party together. Brainstorming with a group is a great idea, but make sure you have the parameters down first so the brainstorm session doesn't get out of hand.

Chapter Four:
Wedding Day Plans

No matter the complexity of your ceremony and reception, it's a good idea to plan it out ahead of time as much as possible. Here are some tips!

A Note on Wedding Planners

Instead of doing it all yourself, consider hiring a wedding planner. While more expensive, a good wedding planner can make your entire wedding experience stress-free. If you want to utilize a wedding planner, make sure she is a good fit for you and understands your needs as a quiet bride. More than likely she is used to brides who want big and loud weddings, but if she is good at her job, then she can easily adapt to your needs and wishes.

You can probably tell right away if a potential wedding planner won't work out for you.

It might be difficult to tell her "no", especially since she would be losing business from you as a potential client. She may try to convince you to ignore your instincts, which is all the more reason to be firm. It might be awkward and uncomfortable to stick to your guns, but do it! Hiring the wrong wedding planner will make your experience *worse* than no wedding planner at all.

A Plan is Good...

Micromanaging isn't. While you want to have a very clear idea of what is going to happen on your big day, you do not need to, nor should you, obsess over a timeline. Things will happen that you don't plan for, so the key when scheduling your big day is *flexibility*. This is important!

Biggest Tip Ever: Remain Flexible!

I can't say it enough. Give yourself plenty of wiggle room. That's another reason why scheduling breaks for yourself is so important, because they also give you a buffer, which reduces stress. Give *yourself* extra time, because even if you're on time, others may not be! Overestimate how long everything will take, because it will probably take longer than you plan. It's much better to have an impromptu five minute break from being early than having to cut your lunch short because you're running late.

Don't wing it. Please, please, *please* don't say things like, "We'll figure it out as we go along," or "I'm sure XYZ won't take *that* long." You'll stress yourself out and probably stress everyone else out, too, which will make you even more stressed.

What to Include in Your Plan

If you don't have a good estimate of how long things will take, time them out beforehand. Then, add a little more time!

- ℘ Preparation: makeup, hair, manicures etc. You probably want to give yourself at least two hours, even if you're doing all your prep yourself.
- ℘ Getting dressed: depending on how complex your gown is, plan *at least* half an hour to an hour just to get in your gown and place all your accessories.

- Transportation: if possible, drive the routes beforehand. Keep in mind possible delays due to construction or accidents.
- Ceremony: the average ceremony runs 30-45 minutes, but try to go through the ceremony ahead of time to see just how long yours will take. Then add fifteen to thirty minutes for any surprises.
- Photography: depending on your package and who you are working with, this can take anywhere from half an hour to three hours or more. Always overestimate, especially if you're planning breaks during your photo session.
- Receiving line: the amount of time this will take will depend on the number of guests. It also depends on the kinds of people your guests are! Some receiving lines speed right along because people are hungry, other times they're slow because each guest feels the need to congratulate you for five minutes.
- Dinner: *at least* an hour. It depends on the kind of meal you're having. Caterers can run late, waiters can be slow, or guests don't seat themselves promptly, so overestimate.
- Dance / Party: How long do you want it to last? You can wrap things up after an hour or two, or

party long into the night if you wish. Just have a clear idea of how you think you'll be feeling at that point (more than likely you'll be exhausted, but you could have an adrenaline rush and feel completely energized!)

- Breaks: remember to schedule yourself fifteen minutes every two hours or so throughout the day to help clear your mind and reenergize.

- Anything and everything else! Depending on your ceremony, your religion, your culture, or your wishes, you may have other important things to do on your big day. Don't forget about them, and plan accordingly.

Summary

You may want to purchase or make a wedding organizer or planner to help keep everything in one spot. Organization helps reduce your stress, but it also makes life easier for everyone else involved in your wedding.

Chapter Five:
Lots of Little Things
to Lighten Your Load

Whether or not you're sticking with more of the bride-centered traditions or taking some of the suggestions in this book to heart, there are a lot of favors you can do for yourself to make the big day a bit easier to handle. Because you're a quiet bride, you should consider some of these tips to stay energized, focused, and happy.

Request Reinforcements

If you didn't nominate a personal attendant, find someone! This person, whether she is a close friend or relative, can be a lifesaver. We introverts typically do not rely on others for assistance or care, but in this situation you must accept her help. She can help keep you hydrated and satiated, can help monitor your "recovery areas" so you have a place you can hide for a few minutes, and she can intercept people who need your attention. I'm also going to encourage you to be a bit more vocal about your needs to your bridesmaids. It's their job (and pleasure!) to help make your day a success, so utilize them.

Sometimes the role of personal attendant is seen as strictly honorary, so be sure to be upfront about your expectations, and say it's okay for her to refuse. After all, she'll be taking on a big job! More than likely she'll be very happy to help, though, and it would be nice to give this person a special gift to thank her.

Take it Easy the Night Before

Schedule a rehearsal as early in the evening as possible. If you're hosting a dinner afterword, stick as close to the rehearsal as time allows. Do not overeat at the rehearsal dinner and avoid alcohol during the dinner. You can probably safely indulge in a couple beers or a glass of wine, but you *don't* want to get even a little drunk tonight.

Call it an evening early and find some quiet space. Plan this out strategically ahead of time! Do not share a suite with your bridesmaids, or at least make sure you have your own space if you do.

You'll probably be at least a little nervous, so take a nice, warm bath with some aromatic bath salts or bubbles (lavender is a good one) to relax. Have a half glass of wine or some tea (chamomile or lemon balm are good options) and read a book, listen to music, or just meditate. Keep the TV off.

Once you feel like you can fall asleep, get into bed. Avoid sleep aids (especially if you've been drinking) since they can make you groggy and achy the next day, unless you have a product you're familiar with. Hopefully you'll be able to drift off. For me, the need for a good night's sleep can cause me anxiety and actually prevents me from getting good rest.

Your bridesmaids, friends, and family may expect you to stay up late, so tell them early on about your plans. If they're pushy, tell them you don't feel well (which is *kind of* true: if you don't rest, you won't feel well the next day!) or that you have a headache.

Start the Day Off Right

Most wedding days begin early. Early beauty salon appointments, photoshoots, or nerves can wake a bride up before she's ready. Hopefully you'll have a full night of rest on your side!

If you normally exercise in the morning, your wedding day shouldn't be any different. Stick to your routine to both do your body a favor and give yourself the extra boost that exercise provides. If you don't normally exercise, try a brisk twenty minute walk to get pumped up and clear your head.

Do not skip breakfast; in fact, eat a *very* good breakfast! A healthy mixture of protein, fat, and good carbs (stay away from excess sugar) will keep you full longer and give you the energy you need. An omelet packed with veggies is a good option, or oatmeal with raisins and walnuts. Avoid very salty foods, like processed meats, in order to keep water retention down. Skip the juice and opt for water instead, though be sure to have your normal amount of caffeine in order to avoid withdrawal symptoms.

Stay Satiated and Keep Hydrated

All the prep work in the world is meaningless if you don't take care of yourself first and foremost. Keeping hydrated may mean more trips to the bathroom, but that's no reason to skimp on the water! A typical (sixteen ounce) bottle of water should last you two hours at most. Your personal attendant can help you stay on track, and she can carry around your water bottle and keep it filled.

Additionally, do not starve yourself all day in anticipation of a large meal. Doing that would wreak havoc on your blood sugar, which starts a downward spiral of misery. You could feel faint or weak (and you may actually faint), develop a headache and/or mental "fuzziness", and lower your ability to handle stress.

Snack on low-mess foods such as roasted (unsalted) almonds and other unsalted nuts, bananas, grapes, cheese and (plain) crackers, or mini-sandwiches (sans mustard). Avoid large amounts of sugary snacks because they really don't do much for you. Your personal attendant can keep some snacks on her at all times for whenever you need a bite, and she can keep a compact and mini-toothbrush for freshening up on the go.

Don't let your bridal party go hungry, either, since they could get cranky and cause you stress.

Aromatherapy

You can include some calming herbs in your bouquet, such as peppermint and lavender, or you can use essential oils to help keep the stress at bay. Have your personal attendant or maid of honor keep a scented handkerchief handy if you aren't lucky enough to have pockets in your gown. Whenever you start to feel overwhelmed, signal her for a break and *take one*.

This is important: *do not* wait until you reach the verge of a mental shutdown to take a break—center yourself right at the beginning to avoid going down that road altogether. All you might need is a few minutes of quiet, deep breathing with some calming scents, and you'll probably feel a lot better.

Keep a Secret

There's nothing like a secret confidence booster! Whether you're wearing your favorite Batman underwear instead of lacy lingerie or your favorite cheapie bracelet instead of bridal jewelry, something only you know can give you an extra boost of confidence.

You can also dye the tulle underneath your gown for a secret splash of color!

Those Shoes Weren't Made for Walkin'...

...so wear some that are! Unless you're wearing a shorter gown, nobody will even see your feet. Achy feet affect your whole body and overall just bring you down. Opt for flats, lower heels, or wedges to help give your feet a break, and make sure they fit well! Wear your sneakers if you want to. I've been to a wedding where the entire bridal party wore colorful sneakers.

Whenever you're taking a break, take your shoes off and put your feet up. If you can soak them in a tub of cool water, or have your personal attendant put a cool washcloth or ice pack on them, you'll feel even better.

Prepare for Emergencies

From a broken nail to a broken shoe, and everything in between, you'll feel the most relaxed if you know there's a way to take care of little "emergencies" that will probably crop up. Prepare little sewing kits with the right colors for you and your bridal party. This is something your personal attendant or maid of honor can keep track of.

Additional helpful items include:

- Cash: a variety of bills and change
- Comb/brush, hairspray, and bobby pins
- Compact mirror
- Disposable ice and heat packs
- Earring backs, jewelry clasps, and small pieces of pre-cut jewelry wire
- Eyedrops
- Fabric glue and hem tape
- Hand wipes, moist towelettes, or sanitizer
- Mini toothbrush, floss, and breath mints
- Nude-toned bandages and liquid bandage
- Pain and allergy medications
- Safety pins and straight pins
- Tampons and pads if it's that time of the month, or close to it (stress can trigger your monthly cycle early)
- Tiny scissors: a versatile tool that can take care of a hangnail or a loose thread
- Tissues and cotton swabs

A stylish diaper bag (or other bag) can accommodate everything above and keep it organized. There's also room for your water bottles, snacks, and other supplies. Try to keep everything in one place so it's easier to keep track of.

Treat Yourself

Do you have a favorite goody? Whether it's a bar of chocolate, junkfood, or another favorite, be sure to include it in your emergency bag. It's okay to indulge in your favorite treat in moderation—too much sugar or salt can be bad overall—but a little taste throughout the day will lift your mood and keep you chipper. If you can find a bite-size version, even better!

This is one day that you don't want to deny yourself. Every little bit helps, especially if it's tasty!

Color Therapy

Maybe you were able to choose calming colors for your wedding, but if not, consider finding or creating a soothing space filled with calming colors. Retreat there for your breaks and be soothed by pale blue, green, and aqua.

You can also make color therapy active with coloring books! Adult coloring books are hot right now and many advertise that they are "stress relieving", though any kind of coloring book will relax you. By concentrating on coloring, you force your brain to shut off all the extra processes it has running (you know, that overwhelmed feeling).

Tip: use colored pencils so you don't need to worry about stains.

It's Not ALL About You

You may be the bride, and your guests may focus on you quite a bit, but you won't be the only person garnering their attention. Weddings are a time for relatives to catch up and have a good time together. It's also an opportunity for your friends to hang out and have fun, and maybe make some new friends.

It may help you relax a bit more if you remind yourself that your friends and loved ones are also happy to see each other, not just you. Even though I constantly urge you to focus on your own wishes first and foremost, it may alleviate some stress to think of yourself as "just" a bride. People get married every day, after all!

Summary

Getting through your wedding *can* be fun and low stress. I hope the tips in this chapter help you, but remember that your own methods for keeping calm and happy are probably the best. Stick to what makes you feel good, regardless of convention.

Chapter Six:
Dealing with Dollars

Weddings are becoming increasingly expensive, averaging a whopping $25,000 (though this figure depends on where you are in the U.S.). Whether you and your fiancé are footing the bill yourself (out of pocket or with loans) or if your families are helping out, dealing with the financial aspects of a wedding is very stressful.

Meeting Relatives' Demands

Many times parents or future in-laws will offer to help out, so long as certain criteria are met. These criteria may be made very clear (i.e. "These funds are contingent upon you marrying in Church XYZ") or implied, sometimes vaguely and frustratingly so.

What's a quiet bride to do? We're not very outspoken or demanding, and we tend to go along with others' wishes in order to save heated words. If you can do without the money they're offering, try a simple "No thank you". If they insist, have them read "A Note to Loved Ones" at the beginning of this book.

However, if you really could use the financial assistance, try having an honest conversation. Talking about money can be very uncomfortable, especially if the discussion is with in-laws instead of your own family. Get your fiancé on board and have him join the discussion. It may help to write out what you wish to say ahead of time so you can stay focused and on topic.

Resorting to threats and ultimatums won't do anyone any good. You can avoid making demands, but unfortunately you cannot control others—if you're feeling threatened or bullied, speak up. The person doing it may not even realize how demanding they are, especially if you normally agree with their wishes.

Your Partner's Agenda
You *think* you know what your fiancé wants in a wedding, and you *think* you're on the same page, but before you start planning away, sit down and talk with your fiancé. This may seem obvious,

but it's so easy for a newly-engaged girl to start planning away, sure their fiancé is 100% on board. You can alleviate loads of stress later on by setting these things straight right away:

- ೫ What's your budget and how will you pay for things?
- ೫ Is everything included in one budget? Or do some items, like your wedding gown, have a separate budget?
- ೫ Who will be involved in the ceremony?
- ೫ Where will the ceremony take place?
- ೫ What is the initial plan for the ceremony?

Designate a time after the dust settles, at least a few weeks after the engagement if time allows, and go through everything. Make sure your fiancé knows ahead of time that it could take hours to solidify details — it's not a fifteen minute chat. If needed, you can divide the planning into chunks: ceremony, reception, honeymoon, appointments, etc.

Even if your fiancé insists that you have total control over the planning (if you want it that way), insist right back to him that you need his input. He probably assumes that you'll plan a few things that are obvious to him, like making his sister one of your bridesmaids or that the ceremony will take place at Church XYZ. It's much better to have a discussion before planning, instead of going back and making changes (and feeling hurt or angry).

Money can be a *very* sensitive issue between couples. Experts recommend complete financial transparency between couples intending to marry, especially since money is the number one cause of marital discord. If you're committed to one another, the time to come clean about your hefty student loans, or your fiancé's double mortgage, is *before* you tie the knot. Luckily, couples nowadays are much more transparent than they were a few decades ago, so this might not be an issue for you at all!

Dollars and Sense
Deciding *who* contributes *what* will likely be another awkward area, especially since the traditions of who is supposed to pay may not be practical or ideal. According to tradition, here is who pays for what:

Bride and Her Family
- Ceremony space and any music accompaniment
- All of the bride's clothing and accessories
- Flowers for the ceremony, reception, and bouquets/corsages for bridesmaids and flower girls
- Photography (and video)
- Reception and everything included in it
- Groom's ring
- Invitations, announcements, and programs
- Transportation to and from ceremony and reception

Groom and His Family
- Marriage license and officiant's fee
- All of the groom's clothing and accessories
- Bride's bouquet and going-away corsage, boutonnieres, and corsages for mothers and grandmothers
- Honeymoon
- Rehearsal dinner
- Bride's ring

Bridal Party
- All attendants pay for their own clothing

- Maid of honor and bridesmaids host wedding shower
- Best man and ushers host bachelor party
- Additional parties

You may be aware of financial issues of those involved in your wedding, or you might not be. If someone is hesitant to foot the bill for something, or hasn't volunteered to pay, they may be embarrassed about not being able to afford it. Tact and understanding are key here. On the other hand, they may simply be unaware of the costs that traditionally come with their role.

Summary

Getting everyone on the same page may be tricky, but it's the best way to avoid costly misunderstandings. Hopefully, everyone will do their own research, which is something you can encourage.

Chapter Seven:
The "Quiet Bride" Look

We all know what a bride looks like: white dress, veil, flawless makeup and hair, and a radiant smile. Unless you're celebrating a different culture or are totally flouting convention, your vision of yourself as a bride probably fits with the description above. Here are things to consider when putting together your bridal look. If you already know what you want, feel free to skip this chapter.

A Note on All Dresses

The bottom line is to wear whatever makes you feel both beautiful and comfortable. If that's a white, side-split gown with a plunging neckline, go for it! You need to feel like you belong in your dress, otherwise you'll feel stressed all day long. The right dress for you will feel amazing. If you've ever watched wedding gown reality shows, you know the moment you found "the one". And that's the most important thing, regardless of the advice in this chapter.

Off-White is ON

Bright white stands out the most, especially since no one else will wear it. Choosing ivory, or even light champagne, will mute your presence a little and help you blend in while still looking like a bride.

By the way, you don't have to wear white. You probably know that already, but I thought I'd sneak in another reminder. It's becoming more and more common for brides to wear other colors, or even black.

Keep it Covered

Yes, I'm talking about your cleavage. You may want to look and feel sexy, but cleavage tends to draw eyes. Personally, I'm all for flaunting what you have if you want to, but the truth is that keeping your girls covered will keep more eyes off of you.

Picking a more modest, yet flattering, neckline largely depends on your frame and cup size. Work with your dress consultant to get recommendations tailored to your body type and size. It's totally possible to keep your girls covered and still feel beautiful and sexy!

Symmetry is Safe

Visually interesting dresses that have features such as side splits, asymmetrical hemlines, one-shoulder gowns, or other accents can draw more eyes, for longer periods of time. I keep mentioning that predictability is calming, and the same goes for your gown.

You do not need to sacrifice beauty in order to have a "predictable" gown, you just need to follow a few rules:

ๆ Keep your dress symmetrical in all aspects
ๆ Avoid trendy cuts, materials, and embellishments (something your guests might not have seen before)
ๆ Stick to classic lines

The View from Behind

If you feel comfortable with people looking at you, so long as you can't see them do it, consider a gown that is most visually interesting from the back:

- 𝕭 Low-cut back
- 𝕭 Corset closure
- 𝕭 Interesting straps
- 𝕭 Embellished train

Veiled Intentions

You may feel inclined to cover your face with a large, embellished veil. Don't—this will actually draw attention to your face. Stick with a simpler style in ivory, or a color that goes with your gown.

A Note on Your Appearance

As with your gown, I'm going to encourage you to style your hair and makeup in a way that makes you feel the most comfortable and beautiful, regardless of the following advice. You will feel the least stressed if you feel like you look your best. The tips below will help eyes pass you over, but when your guests *really* look at you, they'll see a beautiful bride.

In addition to the advice below, search Pinterest and the Internet for bridal looks for your specific skin tone and hair color. After you see the wide variety of results, you'll likely have a much better idea of what you *don't* want to look like, which makes it easier to figure out what you *do* want look like.

"Natural" is Nice

It's not unheard of for grooms to request that their brides-to-be use a light hand with the makeup. After all, he's marrying *you* and he wants to be able to recognize you! Princess Kate was celebrated for doing her own makeup when she married Prince William, and they have the best professionals in England to tend to their grooming needs. Therefore, it's perfectly acceptable to look like yourself on your wedding day.

In addition to referring to natural tones in makeup, this also means sticking to your natural features, so if you do not naturally possess black eyelashes, you may want to steer clear of black false lashes, since they will contrast with the rest of your features.

Neutral is Nice, Too

Contrast is visually interesting. If you're fair-skinned, using black eyeliner and red lipstick (classic pin-up girl) may look very nice, but it will also draw attention to your face. Use products that blend in better with your skin tone and hair color. A neutral look is not necessarily the same as a natural look, but both are inspired by your features first and foremost.

The Beauty of Bronze

If you have the right skin tone for it, bronze is a great way to go! Not only will it go nicely with ivory, but bronze tones are flexible and can accentuate without attracting extra attention. Bronze is a more natural shade, but adds just enough shimmer to make your features shine.

Minimal is Mighty

If you do want to go with a more classic or dramatic look, keep a light hand with it to avoid looking fake. A little black eyeliner goes a long way, as does a rich lip color.

This extends to all of your makeup. When in doubt, keep it light. Caking on makeup to hide your insecurities might actually make them more noticeable (unless your makeup is done by a professional). Plus, you may have more maintenance to do throughout the day if it's hot and/or humid.

Liquid Caution

An easy way to keep your look low-profile is to stay away from liquid liners and lip glosses. These create sharp lines and high-gloss points on your face, which draw attention to your features. Opt for powders and pencils to keep your look a little more matte.

A Note on Hairstyles

Nowadays the range of acceptable wedding hairstyles is so wide that you really can do anything you want. From a completely down and loose 'do to a slicked-back up-do, and everything in between, your hairstyle is an easy way to keep yourself comfortable and feel beautiful. As with your dress and makeup, remember to stick to what works best for you, which may not fit in with the advice below.

One easy way to start your hairstyle journey is to do a search for wedding hairstyles, on Pinterest or the Internet. Scroll through and see which styles draw your eye...and avoid those!

Comfortable is Key

Especially if you're planning a long wedding day, a comfortable hairdo can make all the difference. Usually this means fewer pins and other contraptions to keep your style in place, so a "comfortable" style is oftentimes down or half-down.

If you're prone to headaches, seriously consider a less constrained hairstyle. There are dozens of ways to style hair down or half-down while maintaining a classic, or even glamorous, look.

Simple is Safe

If you want to avoid drawing extra eyes, keep your hairstyle simple. A classic way to do this is a low chignon with a couple curled wisps. A messier chignon still looks nice but gets rid of the "sleek" feel. It's a very versatile style that looks great on straight to wavy hair of any color.

A simple style for naturally curly hair is a low braided bun, with a couple curls loose to frame your face. This will contain your curls in a nice way without drawing extra attention. A braided bun also works for straight and wavy hair, but it may draw a little more attention because the braids will be a bit easier to see.

The Dilemma of Dye (and Highlights)

No matter what color your hair is, your natural shade is likely the least noticeable shade for your skin tone. There are exceptions, of course, but if you're considering a drastic change before your big day, here are a few words of caution. If you've been dying your hair for a while and have no plans to change that, or if you feel the most comfortable rocking fire engine red or electric blue, feel free to skip this part.

Staying close to your natural shade, with little to no highlights, will keep your look uniform, which is less visually interesting. That doesn't mean it won't look good! Highlights and lowlights can do wonders for hair when used correctly, but even if they're a little too bright or too dark, your hair becomes more of an accessory rather than a part of you.

If you're serious about staying out of the spotlight, avoid unnatural (for you) colors and keep the highlights and lowlights to a minimum, or avoid them altogether. Giving into the temptation to do something drastic as your last hurrah before married life may make you braver, but it could also cause you stress if it doesn't turn out exactly right.

Summary

You need to decide if you want to look like yourself, or if you need a "mask" to feel comfortable in front of a crowd. In my opinion, it's always better to be yourself, because that's who your fiancé is marrying. However, I understand that sometimes the best armor for introverts is makeup, because it's something we can control that impacts how others treat us. As always, do what is best for you!

Chapter Eight:
Say "Cheese"!

Chances are if you're a quiet bride, you're also somewhat camera shy. More than likely you dreaded picture day growing up because you found it embarrassing. Even if this doesn't sound like you, take a moment to read this chapter for tips on taking pictures, which is an event in and of itself when it comes to your wedding day.

Practice Makes "Perfect"

If you're like me, getting pictures taken (at any level of formality) causes you anxiety and a severe case of self-consciousness. Like I mentioned in the introduction to this chapter, picture day was *the* worst day for me every year from kindergarten through junior year. Surprisingly, I actually felt okay during my senior picture photoshoot, but that's because of a couple of things, one being I practiced!

I decided way ahead of time that I wanted to actually look good in my senior portraits, so I researched online for tips, poses, and other ideas to help me feel and look my best. Not all poses work for everyone, nor do certain "looks". Ultimately, whatever makes you feel like your best probably makes you look like your best, too.

Your photographer will still direct you to pose certain ways, lift your chin a little, etc., but knowing your best angles can help, too. You can go through photos of yourself and see what the "good pictures" have in common with each other.

Finally, just practice. Personally, I'm not a big fan of selfies, but taking pictures of yourself is a very good way to both get comfortable with pictures, as wells as discovering how you can look your best. Alternatively, enlist the help of your fiancé or a close friend and just practice taking pictures. It will, at the least, get you used to it.

Choose a Great Photographer

This is the second reason my senior year photoshoot went well. My photographer wasn't just great at taking pictures, but she could sense my nervousness and was able to help me relax. A truly excellent photographer will bring out the best in you with little to no effort on her, or your, part.

When choosing a photographer, take into account how you feel around him or her. If she makes you nervous, that will probably show up in your pictures. If he doesn't feel professional enough, your doubt will show up, too. Choose someone you can feel relaxed around, but also choose someone who fills you with confidence in her abilities.

Consider a Separate Picture Day

Taking pictures can last for hours. This adds, on average, three to five hours of just posing for pics to your already long wedding day. If you want nice pictures and don't feel strongly about your groom seeing you in your dress before you're married, then seriously think about scheduling a different day for your formal pictures.

Many beauty salons and spas will allow you two styling days, so you can get a preview of what your hair and makeup will look like on the big day. If all of your bridal party is available, this is a good time to schedule your formal pictures. Even if you can't get professional makeup done (and maybe you don't want to), you can still arrange a picture day.

The logistics may be tricky, especially if you want the groomsmen included in their suits or tuxes, but you can at least get some of the portraits out of the way. The more pictures you take ahead of time, the less you have to take on your wedding day. Even if you can only get you and your fiancé's pictures taken ahead of time, you're still saving time on your wedding day. Not to mention you'll have more privacy with your fiancé, which may help you relax in your photos together.

Work with your photographer to see what kind of package she can offer you…or set up a tripod and do it yourself! The formal shots don't require much skill, just do some Internet searches for ideas ahead of time and enlist someone to snap the pictures.

Consider Fewer Pictures

Do you really need thousands of pictures? Nope. The amount of photographs taken at weddings has increased with the "bigger and better" wedding industry push. Half a century ago, wedding photographers would snap a few formal shots and that was it! Chances are your mom and grandma aren't really missing the thousands of pictures they didn't have taken at their weddings.

Opt for smaller photography packages, or take care of the formal or candid shots yourself. Many wedding photographers are rigid on the kinds of packages they offer, since weddings are (understandably) a large part of their livelihood, so you might have a hard time asking for less. They may be more willing to do a formal portrait session on a weekday, since that wouldn't cut into their Saturday business.

Personally, I feel like too many couples get so caught up in taking good pictures of their wedding day that they don't actually take the time and energy to make good *memories* of their wedding day. If you feel like this is true, too, then stick to your guns about the photography. You really don't need two photographers and a videographer documenting your day.

There are several apps available that your guests can install on their smartphones so they can upload their candid shots securely to you. Alternatively, you can designate a social media #hashtag ahead of time if you don't mind making your pictures public. Many people are quite good at taking selfies and detailed shots, so you'll likely end up with many good pictures this way.

Take Breaks

If you're planning on taking pictures the same day as your wedding, or planning on a lengthy photoshoot, do yourself a favor and take frequent breaks! The photographer will probably try to speed you through the shoot, which will exhaust you. They are professionals and can get the right shots fast, fast, fast! But that doesn't mean you have to be on turbo speed, too. Talk with your photographer ahead of time of taking a little breather every fifteen minutes or half hour.

Summary

If cameras cause you anxiety, there are a lot of things you can do to help yourself. Practice, patience, and a great photographer can make all the difference. Give yourself plenty of time to prepare and more than likely you'll end up with beautiful photographs of your wedding day.

Chapter Nine:
Judgment Day

Worrying what others think is a source of insecurity for many people, especially quiet people. One reason we tend to stay quiet is that we're worried about others' opinions of our words, ideas, and beliefs. Your wedding day is a reflection of you (and your fiancé); you're putting yourself, your tastes, and your dreams on display for your friends and relatives. You may be constantly stressing about your guests' opinions, but this chapter is all about how to shake it off and move on.

Honestly, no matter what you do, at least some of your guests will judge you and your wedding day. Since it's going to happen anyway, even if you hire the best professional wedding planner your money can buy, you should ultimately do what *you* want and what makes *you* comfortable.

"Let it Go"

Even if you're as tired of the movie *Frozen* as I am, this is still a good mantra. Say it with me! Let go of your insecurities and anxiety, because there's nothing you can do to sway your guests' nature. Even if your wedding is "perfect", they'll still nitpick at it until they find something that didn't quite please them or go as they thought it should. We all do it, let's be honest. So it's best to accept that it's going to happen regardless of what you do or don't do, and do what you want to do.

How to Handle Insecurities

Maybe it's not as simple as shouting "Let it go!" for you, and that's okay. Many people battle their inner voices of insecurity and anxiety daily, from the moment they get out of bed until they lie down at night, where they toss and turn replaying every single detail.

My own insecurities about my body unfortunately stem from my mother. In truth, she wanted me to look my best, but the way she went about it was to make sure I knew when I *didn't* look nice, instead of positively reinforcing when I did. She never told me directly that I was fat, but in so many words the message still came across. Words like "frumpy" or "stocky" still haunt me in the dressing room to this day, even after I decided I don't care what I look like so long as I feel good.

You can listen to those little voices in your head that make you second guess every decision, no matter the decision, or you can choose to ignore them. Happiness from within is the truest happiness of all, and it has to start with you. No amount of external praise or validation can ever take you to the level of security that internal happiness can provide. Even though I'm much more confident and sure of myself than I was ten years ago, this is something I'm still working on...in other words, you can't expect a change like this to happen overnight.

Quiet brides, you are beautiful, inside and out. The fact that you picked up this book means you're strong and you know what you want. Just because you're quiet doesn't mean you have nothing to say! Whatever your insecurities are about, whether they stem from your appearance, your abilities, or something else entirely, I know you can silence them and bring your wedding dreams to reality.

Find Your Center

If you haven't tried it yet, meditation can be a great way to calm yourself down, focus your energy, and even heal you. Get in the practice of meditating twice a day, about fifteen minutes each session (more is better), to ground yourself in the morning and clear your head at night.

There are several tutorials available online, even guided meditation videos on YouTube, but the gist is to find a quiet space that you feel is *your* space, sit down in a way that is comfortable, and clear your mind using any of the following techniques:

- Focus on your breathing
- Repeat a mantra—"Om" is a popular one, but your mantra can be almost anything that is both relaxing and inspiring
- Focus on an object, whether it's a candle, statuette, or a spot on your wall
- Visualize yourself in another place, such as a beach or mountaintop

ಐ Concentrate on each separate part of your body and relax it individually

There are dozens of ways to meditate effectively, so it may take some time to find the best way. This is why it's best to start meditating months before your big day, so you're well equipped to handle the stress in ways you're familiar with. Take time for *you*, so you can build your mental and spiritual health as much as possible.

Mindfulness — Mini Meditation

You don't have to sit down for fifteen minutes to find your center (though if you have the time, that's the best way to go about it). Throughout the day you can practice *mindfulness* in order to keep stress at bay and keep yourself grounded. Here's how:

ಐ Focus on the present. What are you doing *right now?* Focus on your actions — walking, reading, typing — and how your body is performing those actions. Feel each finger striking each key or each toe hitting the ground.

ಐ Take a thirty second break and really concentrate on your breathing, nothing else.

扩 If you're feeling stressed or overwhelmed, stop! Whatever you're doing, take a moment and empty your mind. If you can leave the environment or task, do so, otherwise get rid of all the mental negativity before continuing.

Think Happy Thoughts

I'm not naïve enough anymore to believe that positive thinking can solve everything (yes, I used to think that), but I do believe that it can improve quite a few aspects of life and also help medications work better. Bear with me while I talk about the more mystic aspects of happiness, because at the least it can't hurt you to try (and at best it *will* help you).

Positivity begets positivity: the more you practice positive thinking, the easier it gets to see things in a positive way. You begin to see that your *reactions* to situations are just as controlled as your actions; meaning, you can exert some control over your emotions. The next time something "bad" happens (i.e. you get a parking ticket, you overdraw on your checking account, or your BFF is mad at you over a misunderstanding), concentrate on your immediate reaction and force yourself to move past it into acceptance.

However, not all "bad" happenings are equal; in fact, traumatic experiences (death of a loved one, loss of a job etc.) should not be treated the same as daily hardships and annoyances like the examples above. Knowing when to move past anger and when to let yourself grieve is all part of emotional intelligence, where positivity is rooted.

Start small. Soon enough you'll be able to "not sweat the small stuff" without any effort at all. Until then, you'll need to make a conscious effort to let the small things slide.

Research does show that positive thinking reduces overall stress, reduces chance and length of illness, and can increase your lifespan. There are several books and websites dedicated to positive thinking (and even "Buy it now!" program scams that you should avoid), but you don't need anything special to get started.

Summary

Frankly, it's impossible to control others and how they treat you, but it *is* possible to control how you react to others. Choosing to ignore negativity and embrace positivity won't only make your wedding day much nicer, but it will make *you* nicer, too.

Chapter Ten:
Tying It All Together

We made it to the end of the book! How are you feeling? Less stressed? Even more overwhelmed? Let's regroup. Throughout this book I tried to encourage you to do what you wish, first and foremost. Realistically, you more than likely won't be able to do everything you wish *and* avoid the spotlight at the same time. My hope is that this book gave you the tools you need to come up with the best solution for you.

One thing that tends to stress people out is a feeling of powerlessness—that things are completely out of their control. This feeling can cause stress, a mental breakdown, or complete apathy. If I wrote this book correctly, then the last thing you should feel right now is powerless! But just in case, here is a reminder about certain parts of your wedding day you can control, and what to do about the other things that you can't.

Things You Can Control

Believe it or not, there are certain parts of your wedding day that you can almost assuredly count on.

ଵ The world won't end before your wedding day! It may feel like it sometimes, but the odds of something catastrophic happening are minute.
ଵ The people close to you. Unless you chose unwisely or someone becomes suddenly ill, you should be able to count on your best friends and family.
ଵ Your outfit. If you gave yourself plenty of time to prepare, then your dress and accessories should all be ready to go!
ଵ Yourself! Unless you take a mind-altering drug, you can count on *you* to be on your best behavior, so long as you followed the advice in chapter five.

Things You Might Be Able to Control

You may be able to influence the outcome of the following through careful planning, however, don't expect everything in this category to go as planned.

 ⅚ Your guests' behavior. Even with color psychology and crowd manipulation, they may just be too excited! However, if you followed the advice in chapter one, it's very likely they'll behave mostly as expected.

 ⅚ Your look. Accidents happen, so it's possible a broken nose or ripped seam could ruin your look, but it's pretty unlikely.

 ⅚ Your schedule. If you gave yourself, and everyone in your bridal party, plenty of wiggle room, it's very likely you'll be able to stay on schedule.

Things You Can't Control

  Unfortunately, there are some things you just have to "let go". No amount of planning, hoping, or praying will affect the following:

 ⅚ The weather. It happens. The best you can do is come up with alternate locations for any outdoor venues, in the event the weather is less than ideal.

- Truly miserable people. We all know at least one person who seems to get no joy out of life except for bringing others down to their level. I'm not talking about depression, I'm talking about the people who choose anger or spitefulness instead of compromise, for example. The best thing to do, should such a person be present at your wedding, is to be kind and brush off any negativity they try to bestow.

- Accidents! Whether the caterer drops a whole pan of chicken kiev or your maid of honor gets in a fender bender en route to the reception, accidents happen. Be prepared for a few surprises and your day will go much smoother.

Time is Your Friend...

...so long as you give yourself plenty of it! The average amount of time to plan a wedding is one year, which is a good amount of time. It may seem like all the time in the world when you're newly engaged, but it takes about that long to do it! If you have less than a year, you may need more help to stay on top of things.

Through Thick and Thin

In your group of friends or your immediate family, you may be the "quiet one". They may be used to you keeping your opinions to yourself, so you may surprise them when you open your mouth to tell them your plans.

Your friends are your friends for a reason, and they'll be there for you if you need them. The tricky part may be asking for help, since we're usually the ones who are called upon to help, or to listen. It's your turn to ask for help (and get it!) and it's your turn to speak up. You can do it!

Share This Book

To help your friends and family understand what you're trying to accomplish, have them read this book, too. It's not that long! They need to understand where you're coming from if they're to help you effectively.

The Most Important Advice Ever

I hope this book was very helpful and that you learned a few things to help make your wedding day a dream come true! However, the following are the main concepts, and I'd be happy if you follow this advice, even if you take nothing else into consideration:

- Be flexible in all things relating to *you*
- Be firm in your wishes and expectations
- Be creative when addressing your needs and concerns
- Be vocal about your needs to friends and family, and utilize their help
- Trust your instincts!

For more advice on wedding planning, please see the list of resources. There are many great books and websites available for you!

Congratulations!

Resources

All of these resources are available online, or you can check your public library or local bookseller.

Brides: http://www.brides.com/wedding-ideas

The Knot Website: www.theknot.com

My Wedding: http://www.mywedding.com/

The Perfect Palette:
http://www.theperfectpalette.com/

Pinterest: www.pinterest.com

Real Simple Weddings:
http://www.realsimple.com/weddings

Books

Keene, Meg. *A Practical Wedding: Creative Ideas for Planning a Beautiful, Affordable, and Meaningful Celebration*. Da Capo Lifelong Books, 2011.

Roney, Carley. *The Knot Ultimate Wedding Planner & Organizer*. Potter Style, 2013.

About the Author

ANITA KNAPP was a quiet bride who almost eloped. After researching endlessly and finally finding some inner courage, Anita decided to trust her instincts and plan the wedding of her dreams, on her terms. Now she's using what she learned to encourage other quiet brides to do the same. Anita has an MLIS and BA, and lives in the quiet Midwest with her family.